JUNGLE AND OTHER POEMS

Also by Alan Dryden:
The Descending Dark

JUNGLE
and other poems

Alan Dryden

The Book Guild Ltd.
Sussex, England

The Book Guild Ltd.
25 High Street,
Lewes, Sussex

First published 1992

Set in Bembo
Typesetting by Hawks Typesetters,
Copthorne, West Sussex

Printed in Great Britain by
Antony Rowe Ltd.
Chippenham, Wiltshire

A catalogue record for this book is available from the British Library.

ISBN 0 86332 668 4

CONTENTS

Jungle

Is it not hot, this jungle where we crawl?
Serpents manoeuvre through the tangled bush
While from lianas colonies of apes
Snatch at the fruits of meekness when they're lush.
The panther's eyes ignite the moving shapes.
The tiger in the clearing waits to maul.

Bark-resin trickles past the vibrant leaves,
Slides on the floor that's sticky underfoot.
We mess our bodies, lighting on its trail,
Tearing our trousers on the rampant root,
Adherents as we are of this mad gaol.
The tacky mesh confines us as it cleaves.

There's no way out. We are appointed here,
To wait the slow distilling of our age
Through camouflages till our souls evolve
Past lacerations, stuntings and bald rage
Beyond this denseness, finally to involve
The mission of a lonely pioneer.

The Prisoner

Held by the rivet of an overlord
Beneath the hammer of his constant word,
Your eye discerns the critical within
The space its only freedom moves between,
Discerns the slight frown and the supple angst
On righteous brows. It seethes as judge amongst
The stiff and brittle gestures of a few
Who would usurp its freedom and construe
A law to further galvanize what's left
Of its indulgence. Once you are bereft
Of all that gives you impetus to judge
The air around your crucifixion nudge
Your neighbouring victim. If he will not praise
The mild endurance of your stauncher phase
Do not shed the burden of your discontent.
The handle's gleaming of your implement
Is what he sees and fears its useful blade.
His own existence was not ready made
Like yours. He had to prove his own selection
By the power that holds you in subjection.

The Consolation of Woman

You smile at me whose life is an offence
Against the One who knocks upon the door.
I melt in the combustion of your glance.
My feet are lifted miles above the floor.
And when I turn replenished from that look
You walk behind me in the avenue
Where leaves I kick are pages of a book
You read like some old bible in the pew.

Dead leaves are scattered by a gust of wind,
Clearing a path for your approaching feet,
Whose resonance makes echoes in my head,
Spreading out in circles like a wound,
And One lets drip His blood whom I must meet
As you and I are led where we are led.

Household

Shoes lie upended on the floor
And trousers crumpled on the chair.
Tobacco smoke hangs in the air.
An apple eaten to the core
Is turning brown inside the bin
Amid deposits of grey ash.
Outside you hear the cold rain splash,
Intensifying to a din.

The baby restless in its cot
Spits out its dummy on the sheet,
Drums on the bars with frigid feet,
Yet still stays rooted to the spot.
It can't turn over, being frail,
And moans on in a monotone.
A sudden whirring of the phone
Halts its fruitless lone travail.

Father reclines on the settee,
Chewing the evening meal's remains
And tries to steep his worn out brains
In books on electricity.
His wife is ironing his pants
With a forced gesture of despair.
Her elbow knocks a jam-pot where
The jolt disturbs a swarm of ants

Under the lid. How did they find
Their way inside? Perhaps the heat
Attracted them in from the street.
Look how they scurry, mad and blind.
The phone whirrs still. No-one gets up.
The effort's too much for this pair,
Aliens caught in a modern snare,
Waiting for the next coffee cup.

Father and Son

After my years of dust I feel again
For you, child, interceder for my lack.
For years I was the ice that bore the strain
Of winter. Now my sheets begin to crack,
And watching you merge with the fecund swarms
Of other children burgeoning to light,
I move to vision through subsiding storms
And grow to the full measure of my height.
Your laughter like a field of leaping hares
Confirms me in a new communion
With nature spirits who convert my prayers
To tactile faith beyond an orison.
Your home removed from house to park and street
Knows no-one alien. Anyone who calls
Is part of the organic free elite,
Is not confined by stern domestic walls.
For you have cut your chains while still so young,
Are featured now in the world's symmetry,
Who like one condemned for years was hung
Upon the gallows of my gravity.

The Common Inheritance

Absence of God defines the loser's stance.
With feelers he moves through significance,
Grazing the thought of every mind he meets,
Presiding shepherd of autumnal streets.
His genius ranges over passers-by
On sturdy wings and yet he will not fly
Toward a summit where he might through guile
Commit the unsuspecting to a trial.
No he would rather dart a purer ray
Against the misdirected and the stray,
Uncloud the features of their frailty
And know the obverse of their poverty.
Their heads like his are circled by a mist.
They wear the glower of the misanthropist
Though he sees that the attitudes they bear
Refer to One who seems not to be there.
Thus he is joined to them in mute appeal
To what prefers to disappear, conceal,
And leave both blind and the initiate
In common quest for the appropriate.

The Guard

Much coveted my gift is to be standing
Here, an open symbol all ablaze.
No urgent thought besetting or expanding
My mind into a metropolitan maze,
But succulent the breeze is to my lips
Where duty is most visibly begun,
Tensed through my uniform to my fingertips,
And for its sustenance always the gun.
My other armaments remain impounded
In rows within the arsenal of my brain
For thought is like a volley to be sounded,
And I must pull the trigger to be sane.
Not that there's interruption to my sights
Which ever horizontal do not veer.
I do not make an issue of my rights
But turn a cheek to my fixation here.
Just now and then an amber-like remorse
Makes me retreat into esprit de corps
Before I hoist my rifle up with force
And know myself a universal law.

Birds, Girls and Drills

The blackbirds, beak-down, stalk the leaf-strewn grass,
Solicitous of what they cannot find.
Lithe teenage girls laugh loudly as they pass,
Dropping their freshly peeled-off orange rind
That's no use to the blackbirds. Noise of drills
Impregnates the air. My mind is slow
To reckon with the heaviness that kills
Its thoughts and poetry that will not flow,
As I score pages with a languid ink,
Too weak to sculpt the image into art.
My fluent lines contract, submerge and shrink
Much like the computations of the heart
When it confronts the blank wall of outside,
And cannot bridge the arid space between.
Like some dead seagull drifting with the tide
It has no strength to counter such routine
The thrust and pull of life prepares for it.
I must revert inside my skull to dreams
And trust the fond impressions that they knit.
Who knows what autism loosens major themes?

The modern alien stance brings the dark near.
We grope like blackbirds for essential food
While laughing girls cannot allay our fear.
Noise of construction infiltrates our blood.

The Museum Attendant

Looking around for someone to engage him,
(Self-doubt was cloistered by unwholesome brick)
The cold apartment barely could assuage him,
His pulsing brain was needled by the tick
Of one gilt pendulum; that alluring swing
Displaced the drifting bodies through the entrance,
And at unguarded instants its brass ting
More than the ticking pierced him like a lance.

He peered out through a fulgent wave of eyes,
No give away of friendship in their laughter.
He shrivelled in his uniform, not wise,
Not greedy for inclusion or dependent,
Still on their graceful fluctuance incumbent,
Beneath the dust that filtered from the rafter.

Man is an object

As linear and formal as the bars
Of street-lamps or the rows of cruising cars,
We walk within the streets of inward sighs,
With thought-rays trained on each the other's eyes,
Contained within a geometric frieze
Under the censure of the weeping trees.

A ready hammer would feel less inclined
To strike its nail than mind clash upon mind,
As now the blood from cells starts to suffuse,
And silently our points of view accuse.
Where lies the fluid object that can make
Each pent-up atom drown within its lake?

The alien whole conditions every part
To cauterize each gesture of its heart
Till that heart bleeds a rust that fast corrodes
Its pity to gratuitous pleasure-modes,
A pleasure that rejoices in the pain
Its flow inflicts in smearing stain on stain.

Until our gait so cramped and so alone,
Unforced, no longer knows it as its own.
We're insects at the mercy of the air,
Almost invisible as she is there.
We hold the stage, enacting the same role
Of visitant extra-terrestrial.

Anonymous

To spend our days anonymous to light,
The city's magnet, strangers who implore
Us to the artifice of what is right
In terms of custom, always to do more

Than plane the jagged edges of existence
And keep within its stark parameters,
Is this not meet for an ordained persistence,
Obedience to a parent who prefers?

In childhood something called us to adjourn
The case our corporate spirits would pursue.
We acquiesced but later to return
To factors unresolved under review.

Now all that we purport to signify
Is water trickling over broken stones,
Not caring that a thirst should wonder why
We only answer with our rippling tones.

It is our element to be unmoved
While journeying toward an end unknown,
Static and vacant like a child unloved,
Until he holds the gift of being alone.

Flagstones

You, bristlers with the pounding of the lost,
And many whom the weight of their disdain
For those who with them steam beneath the rain
Makes them lean away or risk too high a cost,
Of such you are the living sacrifice.
The dust from their oppressive posturings
To your prostrate, static forbearance clings.
Transfixed, you measure out their artifice.

Yours the relief when one child jumps for joy.
You feel as if a secret, unused limb
Were spiralling to heaven from the flat,
And when two, arms linked, stationary, coy,
Use you awhile, she subservient to him,
It's with you, you feel, they're stopping for to chat.

The Invalid Girl

Content to bear the weight of your distress,
Reclining in the comfort of your chair,
You watch those navigate your lone duress
Who adumbrate a loftier despair,
And wonder what possession they're concealing
That moulds them in a stance so resolute
As though by harder witness they're revealing
Something more testing and more absolute.
Your blanket flutters but you do not shiver,
Not since the frissons of uncanny night
Bound you in secrecy to be the giver,
Watcher and co-transmitter of the light;
That force that telescopes from your mild eye
To energize and yet secure salvation
For one it hits and mitigates his 'I'
And draws him into harrowing relation,
Who now admits that all he has desired
Is to obtain permission for in-seeing
And now upon the pearl he has admired
Projects his entire hitherto veiled being.

A Scaling Down

A working day complete, the mind is tired
Of contradictions which its routine wired.
The evening brings a slow suffusive void,
Like tungsten that in heat is being destroyed,
Reducing its solidity to soot.
The carpet's thick pile irritates the foot.
A fly trapped between curtain and the pane
Recalls the locked wards of the blank insane.
The buzzing stops. The heart intensifies.
Acidic tears begin to smudge the eyes.
What's happening to the will, that branching oak,
Disintegrating like the coals I poke?
When will the garden rose cease to accuse
Disinterest with a Nature I abuse?
I used to love the cherry's flooding bloom
Till colour-blindness sealed me in my room,
And though I scent the perfume of the flowers
Upon the mantelpiece the clawing hours
Of clock beside them tear my spirit's frail
Close-threaded tapestry with their travail.
The printed word turns watery in its line.
My intellect's adulterated wine.
I pull my slippers on and feel them knit
Round toes benumbed by draughts. They cramp then split
The slippers' fabric. Thus my socks protrude.
An ugliness accentuates my mood.

The Post-Mortem Visionary

He stares through features in a jaundiced light
That shimmers round the wandering silhouettes.
No spiky nerves twitch from them. Strings are tight-
Supporting on the loose-limbed marionettes,
Enacting a charade to our observer,
Who sees into their pliancy of soul
With eyes of ferret tumbling the fervour
His mind appropriates from each star role.
For one plays Hamlet, one Macbeth, one Lear.
All fit the designation of their fate
While he planes over them, the cautious seer,
And almost know their deaths' appointed date,
And what awaits them after they have passed
Into communion of a shaded cast.

The Old Narcissist

The pipe, the knife, the matches are in place.
He coughs and rises from his rocking chair,
Forsaking pleasure for the mirror where
He greets the living demon in his face.

At first appalled by what confronts his stare,
The brow stern, oily in the watery light,
An eye that terrifies him with its sight
And rage spelt in the agitated hair.

He turns abruptly to reveal a beard
Of ashen silver in its profile, hem
As sheer as any lightning stroke of nem-
Esis that draws him closer to the feared.

Conclusion. Plucking at the white spines so
He intones madness in a dirge-like hum,
And vainly tries to smoothe with swift crooked thumb
The whiskers to an ornate furbelow.

But ceases when he finds they still protrude.
Nothing can save him whose persistent gaze
Confirms the features that he would erase
Before the grave exerts its finitude.

The Meal

Partaking of the meal in silence, they
Surveyed each other's movements with the knife.
One poked his steak indignantly. It lay
Protruding from the plate's edge, futile life,
Now tattered and misshapen as if death
Had left a final manna to distil
In air that circulated like a breath
Around this lump of broken flesh to fill
A space where he, this silent eater, cut
It piecemeal into strands till juices ran,
Persuading him that life was in it yet,
But still too rare to satisfy the man.
    His onlooker passed to his second course.
    The silence reigned about them like a force.

The Avatar

In crowds he stalks through book-shops and cafes,
And bears the brunt of fashionable displays
In chain-store windows. Almost in a trance,
And almost naked to the world's advance,
He wants to root himself, forbidding oak,
And stem the tide of life's presumptuous joke.
Like Caesar with an arbitrating thumb
He seeks to hound the city with a drum,
And banish the encroaching artifice
Until the streets and thoroughfares are his.

But short of that his sly unconscious mind
Obliterates the pompous and refined,
That he might focus on the crucial need,
Veiled in the spaces occupied by greed.
For if he could erase self-interest
And bring to bear his being on the rest,
Who peck amongst their refuse in the bins
He might achieve the transference of sins
By first subsuming them so that one sees
Him grow transparent with the world's disease,
And stand a cancerous monstrosity,
One who reversed the bonded and the free.

The Cup of Water

He watched the water circling in the cup
Until it slowly came up to the rim.
The swirling bubbles settled at the top.
The tap turned off, the pipes began to hum.

So measured and composed had been the fill,
He feared to drink in case he would derange
A quantity replete, so cool, so still
And sacrosanct, it seemed a crime to change

Its level. Yet his lips were tempted to
Usurp the order in the vessel now,
Those lips that knew how they were breaking through
A chastity that could not take a vow

Forever to remain untouched because
It was not water in a holy font,
A consecration under sacred laws.
Simply a thing a thirsty man could want.

Just then a breeze ruffled the surface and
A droplet overtopped the porcelain.
He could not say what omen had been planned,
Should he consume or pour it out again?

That droplet trickled like a silent tear
From an enraged and agitated face.
He left the cup together with its smear
And went into his room to beg for grace.

The Need for Preference of Another

I want you placed right here before my face,
That I might find my true location where
No doors suggest departure to the dank
Formless exterior devoid of grace.
The reticence of you here by my chair
Is all the quaint illusion I could thank.

And if not you then something else before me,
Some imprint like your name personified
Into a shape bold in its symmetry,
That when the daily destinies ignore me
It might through fondness be transmogrified
Into atonement's fitting poetry.

Without you here to witness I am weak,
Fretting against the shadows that appal,
The moonlight clamouring against the pane.
If there were listeners I'd surely speak
Of spores of selfhood free and terminal,
And those who bear the poison of their stain.

Outside the Poem

To go beyond the word to some fine tone
Is what the poem urges and demands.
The choicest pasture in all conscience sown
By self-effacing, piano-playing hands
Must yield abundance for the starving mind,
Which tuned beyond all detriment to nerve,
Might capture what the great performers find,
And prize like a possession fit to serve.

The writer ceases, loses now the more,
Teasing from silence something like a sense,
An instant, dark, that speaks of a before.
He hears eternity inside his thought
And stands outside his work as in a trance.
A shower of grace notes echo their report.

The Nursing

Blank days that pass before amorphous eyes
Give nothing but familiar lineation.
One might as well drift through an endless mist
Down to a derelict, ramshackle station,
Or go to halls where money-men devise
A dreary spectacle of flesh and fist.

And so a life is filtered through the sweep
Of what a common heritage ordains,
A death that's master-minded by a force,
Oblivious to the undercurrent's pains
Where all those born of unsuspecting sheep
Career together on a deviant course.

Until one from the prison of his plight
Sees something at a tangent on the weight
That bears towards his tender pliancy,
And finds the words amid attack to state
The cause and remedy of this cold blight
To nurse a hope for future progeny.

The Swans

I lay my head upon the pillow while
Two swans enter the slipstream of my thought.
The trees upon the farther bank beguile
Their fond attention at this languid sport
Where leaves seem to suffuse a varied light
Upon those swans' backs and I turn to see
Their heads dip in the water where the tight-
Held instants of these images agree.

Then one emerges, water draining down
The rigid figuration of her beak.
The other goes on probing with the deep
Determined perserverance of the clown
Before a lone spectator, as I seek
The reason why I cannot sink to sleep.

The Typist

You tread the streets each morning with a smile,
Your corn-stalked hair just ruffled by the breeze,
Between two rows of trees that seem to file
In tempo with your nonchalance and ease.
Why should you hurry when the impetus
To work begins when you have settled in
To tea and biscuits and the usual plus
Of hair adjusted in the mirror's grin?
I picture your deft fingers in the tray,
The slightly parted lips revealing teeth,
Grim and prepared for the efficient day,
For sheets of carbon, letters underneath;
Your sufferance of small-talk in the pool,
And now and then back-biting, cattiness,
But always the adherence to the rule
Of satisfying the beleaguered boss.
No doubt at noon it's crispbread that you eat
And extricate the crumbs from your corsage,
Thinking how sometimes other hands repeat
The selfsame motion in a slow massage.
But that is planned for strictly after hours
With an acquaintance in a higher bracket,
Always the bearer of exquisite flowers
And other gifts to complement your packet.
So when at six I listen for those shoes,
Formal, assertive, past my window's view
I think that they reveal essential clues
Of what a liaison would mean with you.

Two-Way Stretch

Excluded from the Other's opening arms,
I'm thrown back on my own supporting heels,
Debarred from those forthright prescriptive charms,
A fixture somewhere deep within me reels.
Suspension's what I aim for, just enough
To keep me straight against the looming week.
I file the polyps in me that are rough,
That I might take off without jolt or creak.

But in the outer reaches that await
And beckon with a broad insidious hand
Are positive obstructions to my style,
Fibrous indecencies that cling and grate
Against my sensibilities like sand;
A summons and an overwhelming trial.

Chains

Whole textures of black earth assert their weight
And block the air-shafts under which I heave.
I thrust and kick in this dark foetal state
And hear my mother up above me grieve.

Colossal is the pressure from all sides,
Cementing gradually into a block.
Amidst this pattern of relentless tides
Imperatives and questions interlock.

Why am I staved for nothing I have done?
You must submit to force of circumstance!
Why are my senses shaded from the sun?
You can't expect an answering response!

Before the booming voice that designates
I suck what's left of former sustenance
Until a hand drops paltry surrogates,
And what is real food seems a thing of chance.

The thought appals me that this must go on,
And that a grown-up world has sanctioned it.
But what will be the view when flowers are gone,
And space and time by apathy are lit?

Two

I hardly know you, and I hardly know
Myself. Must we two strangers then conspire
To stage a sad, ridiculous dumb-show,
Then plunge into a more consuming fire?

Who'll be our witness when presented thus,
When our two spirits seldom intertwine,
Leaving a stark residual overplus
Of desolation we must countersign?

Shall we retreat within our minds to where
Some concept lifts us clear beyond our plight?
How then shall two mind-readers, debonair,
Disclaim the impulse that confirms our night?

A night progressive in its shadowed reach,
No end or aperture to grope toward,
But echoing with some eternal screech,
And we constricted on its tightening cord.

He who is no longer

He was a man whom many souls could like,
Like what he wrote, licked by the tongues of hell,
A lovely troubadour whom Satan's strike
Sent paraplegic down a soaking well.
And not alone. His songs accompanied him
To echo back to daylight up above,
Encircle kindred folk on the world's rim
And heat them with the oil he breathed called love.

Unique, a personality, a djinn,
He should have been located everywhere
With smiles sufficient to release his chains,
But shadows from old flames came stealing in
To turn his living strength into despair,
Melt down his harmonies to shy refrains.

Is London Sick?

Is London sick? Or must things be this way
Where streamlined bodies rush towards their end?
Yet there's no end. The scene begins next day.
The actors aren't for real but just pretend.

Not from an inner spark do these perform,
But driven by some lean seducer's hand.
They are as bushes bent within a storm,
Whose strength they neither feel nor understand.

If one should not be merely dazed but axed
Others would go on eating at their table,
And view the horror in a style relaxed,
Like horses munching oats within a stable.

Relationship with Nature means divorce.
Bird, animal and bee are mouth agape.
The lake's a cauldron of repressive force.
The cloud disintegrates into no-shape.

No wonder there are beggars in the streets.
No wonder no-one offers them a crust
While intermittently the wind repeats
Its rendez-vous with refuse and with dust.

At night the streetlights turn their jaundiced stare
Upon a mausoleum of vacancy.
The bodies that once occupied the air
Are drowning in a livid molten sea.

The Child in her House

And now the child's cold fingers grip the pin.
I see her turning to the moonlit stair.
No grace, but all the tawdry world therein.
Watch how the light's impressions hold her there,
Stunned before the suctions of tomorrow.
Her cheeks palled by the curtains of self-doubt
When all she wanted was to ask and borrow.
So easy, quick the formings of her pout.
Nobody stands to wait, superintend
Behind her where the door infects her fear
Where floor and carpet do not seem to blend
Into a solace. Chests of drawers are queer
With silence. Still the kitchen holds its smell,
Wherewith the cat's indifference is complete.
A mile away the church's ailing bell
Speaks of its sickness where the huntsmen meet.
Out in the air the fox and weasel shake
In frantic harmony against their doom.
The child thinks of a water-lilied lake
Although her future reckons with a room
Where nylons, lace contain infinity,
And what will be decided when beyond
She sees lacunae where divinity
Shapes reachings in its pale autumnal frond.

The Friends

He lived inside a small community
Where friends would almost queue to bring him out,
Clean-shaven youths (he would avoid the lout).
His needs were met within their company.

In fact they formed a federal paradigm,
Mechanics of a revolutionary clock
That ran with a pronounced and smooth tick-tock.
It seemed the prototype of future time.

The close-knit bunch intended to be seen
By those who still protracted their hard day
Into an evening's featureless display
Of sofa'd bodies inches from the screen.

They were indeed held up to scrutiny.
Some thought them clearly chic or avant-garde,
Destined to disintergrate like lard.
For others they were too select and free.

They used to sport a similar brand of tie,
Not like a school but merely to impress
The elegant with soberness of dress,
A pattern with which many could comply,

Or so they wished. It was by such a sample
They hoped to generate a vital change
And gradually, successfully estrange
An element that feared their fond example.

The Sadness Induced By Women

She lowers her gaze at what seems an affront,
Or is it simply female modesty?
Against such magisterial looks you're blunt,
Shorn of all warmth, self-love and potency.
A guilty fish whose glum descending eyes
Are locked in tempo with her eyebrows' rise.

What chemistry of mind's tampered with thus,
Emotions twisted into panic dread?
You're debited while she disports her plus.
Language devolves to what remains unsaid.
Reason deserts you, thought's unkempt, dishevelled.
And still her mystery is left unravelled.

What freak gave rise to that instinctive turn
Away from what once held you and admired?
She's cold as snow while you're the tapering burn
That could explode the sticks to which you're wired.
No doubt some latent purpose she perceived.
The more you probe the more you're self deceived.

It's final. No remark can make redress.
The cleavage aggravates the smouldering shame,
And though you want two smiles to coalesce
It's no use waiting. You're the one to blame.
A sexual cul de sac is now at stake
As you in blankness contemplate her wake.

The Clock

The clock with pointers resolute at nine
Imposes its fond silence on the room.
It stands where past and future intersect,
And slowly holds the present in its line,
As if a child were growing in its womb,
And nurturing what no-one can detect.

But now its telling index is displaced.
The hour has re-emerged in a new phase.
We watch its purpose formally dictate
Tonight's decisions, ones we've hardly faced.
We're still prone to postponements and delays,
Hesitant before some stroke of fate.

The pointers move to no climactic end.
They will continue on their course when we,
Nervously reluctant in our will,
Have halted time by instinct to forfend
The thought of losing our security,
That dream we'd hoped the clock's hours would fulfil.

The Priesthood of the Believer

When strictured in the silence of his room,
Like Cuthbert genuflecting at a tomb,
He lets the shrill frustrations of his years
Distil their pressure in a bath of tears,
Cleansed by the stab of this climactic point,
Now he feels new sensations that anoint.

His head turns to the window in a jerk,
As if ignited by a spurting spark.
Oak branches are convulsing in the wind,
Like palsied ones constrained by a demand
They must obey. He thinks of Aaron's rod,
Activated by the mind of God.

He knows he must with diligence refill
The ailing vessel of himself and will
His body and his fraught mind to repeat
The instruments of faith he must complete,
That he might stand in tune with what's divined,
And finish designator and designed.

He looks in fond surveillance at the earth,
Not sure of what its remedies are worth.
Then just beyond the dim extremities
He hears a something trailing in the breeze,
The comforting expression of a note,
And feels a summons rising in his throat.

The Touch of Home

The blind man who with bird's composure treads
Through autumn leaves back to a door he feels
With a prehensile finger that he guides
Around the keyhole where the paintwork peels
Seems to detect the world is watching him
To see if he's succeeding as he tries
Amid the shadowed obelisks that brim
Around his childlike, blank revolving eyes.

With pride he does not falter on the step,
Takes time to size up and caress the key
While from his smile gleam two white sets of teeth,
The upper denture biting on his lip,
Until in joy the door's unlocked and he
Enters, clean as a knife into the sheath.

One goes down

One goes down to tips and gutters,
Street-refuse, forbidding bridges,
Listening to perennial sputters,
Smooth luncheon-talk, click of fast heels,
Folds within himself and pledges
Existence in just how he feels.

When freedom's reached its sharpened point,
And there's no strength to scale the gates
Our ferret-eyed one will anoint
His family with simple words,
And meet the schoolteacher who states
Air, water, earth were made for birds.

I Had You Once

I had you once, but lost you in the dark.
You left me in a prison without eyes.
I am the vagrant locked within the park
Where overhanging trees block the sun's rise.
I'm left to fidget like one with a tic.
The world's abysmal motion is my food.
My consciousness is female tights that click,
Anatomies that tempt me to the rude.

I sense that they take pictures of me here.
The shutter falls from each accusing brain.
I am the wounded fox that gnaws his legs
Within the trap of innocence and fear,
Inured to my affliction, but the pain
From those I bear who shun the one that begs.

The Dog of the Gate

The terrier's eyes fix steadfast on the gate
As humans' on an altar or a shrine.
If feet crunch on the gravel soon or late
He'll cock head like a bottle pouring wine,
And let the much-loved owner freely pass
Into the sanctity of his domain
Without a bark or lurch upon the grass,
But like a statesman proud before a train
Of visitors he's welcomed up the drive
From where conviviality begins.
This creature though is reticent to enter
A house that's neither vacant nor alive.
He halts from following and almost grins,
Then reassumes his circle and its centre.

The Man with Feelers

He's almost married to the world before him.
He sucks in each loose person to his core.
Nobody, once encountered, can ignore him.
His lithe antennae curl to their own law.

So sensitive, he licks at every nerve
And fibre of another's supple being
Until it's fitted like a photograph
Inside his membranes, so he's always seeing

The form and nature he'd reconstitute
With cleansing fluid to a perfect whole,
Adding one more playing card to his suit,
Another button to his desk-control.

The Pure Response to the Pure Two

How you survey those two kissed faces there,
Like quartz rinsed in an endless tidal flood,
Mosaic where no bead is out of place.
One from her brow clears a stray wisp of hair.
Another shows the Passion and the Grace,
Both waxed as leaves on each side of the bud.

So pure to one for whom perfection means
No trace of judgement in his avid stare.
The two might be seraphic from their birth,
Sent precious ones a timeless mother weans,
Confides with a fond mission to the earth,
Like one who since the Cross has nurtured care.

Or is it that these two pre-date the world,
Reflections of a morror held beyond
Where all is patterned in eternity,
As stitch by stitch a robe is plained and purled
To clothe the shipwrecked in the murky sea,
A brief to which the wandering respond?

The Benighting

The stones stained by the rain are tinged with grey,
Depressing to the house-bound lady's eye.
Their sight brings early shadows to her day,
And she is soon disposed to question why
This vision should encroach upon her life,
A telling door that slams upon her face,
Or thug that threatens her with unsheathed knife.
She starts up from her chair and drops her lace.
A needle pricks her ankle as it falls.
Her time is racing anti-clockwise back,
As though a swarm of flies came through the walls,
And pictures, ornaments turned to attack.
Through rage she does not move, she is ice-bound.
What sentence from above has come to pass,
Compounded by the absence of a sound,
What jaundiced light is filtering through the glass?
She reaches for some token of support.
Her arms take on the guise of semaphore.
She shouts into the void, a tide's retort
Whispers incessantly upon her shore.

One Night

Since nothingness had issued from his prayer
He tossed within the bed and kicked the sheet.
Tricklings of sweat descended from his hair.
There was no essence his desire could meet,

Except a narrow gorge through which his mind
Was guided like one urging a small pin
Through matted fabric, afterwards to find
A void its lone progress was centered in.

What could it do but lurch from side to side
In automatic palsy till its strength
Was dissipated in its own ebb-tide,
And like a swimmer in his final length

Feels all the weight of failure in his arms,
That slacken just before he makes the end,
Want of achievement set off all alarms.
No seconds for the time-keeper to lend.

Fatherless the orphan sank his head
In pillows till the morning's early chill
Detailed the day's scenario ahead,
And quantified the spaces he would fill.

The Stubbornness

A row of patient slippers on the floor,
Thick-deniered stockings rising to the knee,
Their lives eroded to the apple-core,
The inmates sit in wait on the settee.

In wait? No, they're just reading through the past.
Events are tumbling on a film spooled back.
High moments send their pulses throbbing fast,
And no-one seems too maudlin through the lack

Of love she once experienced. Now her state
Is to be helped in sleeves and given tea,
And ushered to a table and a plate,
Thus galvanized to a docility

Though in an awkward time she may contort
Her mouth in vengeance and bleat like a sheep
Until the others view it as a sport,
Or one complains it keeps him from his sleep.

It's only to demand the sister's time,
And call attention to discomfort if
Her handkerchief's too tight along her arm,
So she can't pull it down to have a sniff.

The House

One roof juts out above the others there,
An all-forbidding stark inverted v,
As if a magistrate had raised his brows,
And one on trial now could not guarantee
Impartial judgement, sweating in his hair.
The mind dwells on a very private house.

Two birds shoot from the chimney-stack as though
They'd felt a vibrant shudder from inside.
Since no-one exits we must still suppose
The members of the family abide
Within a spun cocoon in which they know
Nothing external robs them of repose.

No milk lies on the step, no postman knocks.
Neighbours who watch for life from day to day
Are disappointed that the curtains are
Forever open. Surely he's away,
Or else engaged in crime behind the locks,
As incognito as a film-star.

But no-one ventures to see if he's dead,
The owner who has hibernated long,
Or if at night he surfaces, a mole,
Commits a trespass or some other wrong.
It's clear how man prefers himself instead,
Shrinks from the touch, a hand from the live coal.

The Bay-Window Opposite

The window starting from the mottled brick
Stares at the languor in the poplared street.
Absence lurks like a bomb with measured tick
Where curtains hide the moods of the elite.

What mannered reverence they must cultivate,
On whom no salesmen, callers, thieves intrude.
The window, life-long pristine celibate
Dispels contamination like a prude.

When once I saw a figure from the past
Gaze hands on hips out through the lattice-frame
It was as if my being had trespassed
Overtly on a private, hallowed name.

One winter when the imprint of the frost
Made looking out impossible, opaque
I thought the glass would splinter in disgust,
And cause the whole establishment to quake.

But now I see how regal and controlled
It stands, commissionaire to welcome light,
As if its purpose were to bless, uphold
A family whose every step is right.

The Artist's Wife

That pained expression on your face tells me
That shadows have descended on your soul.
A seed has not matured upon your land,
And you, downcast, forsake this territory,
A pony that rejects its sickly foal,
Wave that disintegrates upon the sand.

Your easel, palette stand in the cold room.
The drape hangs like a cloud incised by storms.
Your canvases are coated with a must
That gathers on a long neglected tomb
While features you once laboured to give forms
Stare out like ghouls caparisoned in dust.

You do not eat the nutriments I cook.
Your body sags, your shoulder-blades protrude.
You lumber round the house a broken jade.
Your past crowning achievements you forsook.
Disinterested you sink into a mood,
A fond recording scratched and overplayed.

Where is the fury born of primal lust
When I disrobed and posed in innocence?
You loved the contours of my body then.
Now naked I'm the hub of your disgust.
You look on me as if I'm an offence,
As if I play the hag within your ken.

Tabula Rasa

Like a dog that's just gathering speed,
He turns from the volumes he's read,
And abdicates poem and creed
For the harvest of living instead.

He finds a stout tree by the bank,
Climbs it and observes the sleek spate
Of minnows, swift darts he can thank,
And dreams of a swarm through the state.

A furnace consuming the bone
Of all that obstructed his way
Is what he invents when alone,
Commits to the construct of day,

No more than a shape to him now,
But soon to be fleshed out, preferred
With the changes the few will allow,
For they are receivers who've heard.

Rose on the Shelf

Rose against whose pallor looms the wall,
So neat upon your shelf and in your bowl
The water slowly draining through the stem
While petals that, obedient to the call,
Not to distort the round perfected whole,
Stand as if circling air protected them.

You who return the watcher's steadfast gaze,
Not shy but resolute as if you knew
The worries that pollute his complex brain,
Fill the depleted hedges of that maze
With growth abundant, he cannot eschew
Your properties that mitigate his pain.

You wait out the duration of your lease,
As fixed as light from stars that never fail
Until you slowly decompose with grace,
Envisaging the moment that you cease
Will be like someone's leaving of a gaol
To blossom in an unknown radiant space.

Incommunicado

Since he has fallen to routine of learning
She settles by the fire, wool on her lap,
Caught in a feelingless unconscious trap,
A lump of coal resistant to its burning.
Real nourishment eludes him in his quest.
He only wants to navigate his way
Amid the reefs that loom upon his day.
He wants the contours of his life expressed
In clear defining words. She knows her smile
Cannot unravel vital skeins that bind
Together in the forest of his mind.
Her breast and lips no longer reconcile.
    Apart, inhabiting respective spaces,
    The single route of life's mapped on their faces.

Too much I see of night

Too much I see of night, its molten pitch,
A half-crazed girl that tugs at every stitch.

The moon hangs like a sour lemon where
Night-watchers pull a wry face at its flare.

Eyes haunt me, open casks of jewels in
This chamber sultry in its pride of sin.

A prowler stops to light his cigarette,
Victim of teacher, lawyer, martinet.

I smell the drop of ash upon his sleeve,
The only saving grace he can conceive.

Late vendors clank their barrows down the street,
The smell of hot-dogs wafting to their feet.

If Satan walks he dances more when passed
By tarts and lovers operating fast,

And others mooching round until its time
To cock the trigger, consummate the crime,

Determined by their blindness to the real,
Existing by the static that they feel.

The rain starts. By the dockyards the lean hounds
Are stamping out their sentence in their pounds.

Coffee-House Event

The Italian women filled the air with talk.
The Chinese girls, impassive, sipped their drink.
Each mind tried to discern the other's thought,
Causing the space between their seats to shrink.
The cafe seemed a net where we were caught,
Our common factor click of knife and fork.

Then he stood stark within the doorway's frame
In tattered jeans like a contemporary saint.
He strode towards the counter with a cough
That nearly brought the waitress to a faint.
He gave a smile then tore his jacket off.
Tattoos gleamed on his chest with Jesus' name.

'D'you think you're saved, you pagan trash,' he screamed.
'You gormless crew of bland indifference.
Perhaps you don't know that He's coming too.
How will He ever banish your offence,
He who suffered from the likes of you,
Who have no chance in hell of being redeemed?'

The general consternation of the room
Could not admit of laughter or the jeers
That peal on football terrace every week
Though someone said, 'He's just one of those queers,
Religion has transformed into a freak.
They say it's all predestined in the womb.'

He stood half naked in his glory though
No halo circled round his punkish hair,
An ancient prophet with a modern style,
A macho star with an angelic air,
Elect to put humanity on trial
And seal its bond with Satan down below.

He yelled, 'I won't be seeing you again,
Not in the life I'm bound for, no not there,
You might as well prepare to meet your fate.'
And so he left them with malicious stare,
With power still to hold, reverberate,
From one who'd been conspicuous of men.